Romans

Trust the Faithful God

Sarah K. Howley

Flaming Dove Press

Romans: Trust the Faithful God (Large Print)

Flaming Dove Press
an imprint of
InspiritEncourage LLC
1520 Belle View Blvd #5081
Alexandria, VA 22307
www.inspiritencourage.com

ISBN 978-1-960793-45-4 (e-pub)
ISBN 978-1-960793-46-1 (paperback)
ISBN 978-1-960793-47-8 (large print)

Printed in the United States of America

Library of Congress Control Number: 2026906124

Contents

Welcome

to this Study of Romans

Paul penned this letter to the Romans around 57 A.D., likely while he was in Corinth (modern day Greece) during his third missionary journey. He had travelled widely by this time but had not yet visited the Roman believers. His letter served as a theological introduction to the gospel he preached.

The believers in Rome were a diverse group. Some were Jewish and others were Gentiles; they came from a variety of different social statuses and jobs, bringing with them different cultural backgrounds and varying familiarity with the Scriptures. As they learned to follow Christ together, much like modern Christians, they found themselves wrestling with questions. They needed clarity on topics like righteousness, obedience, grace and whether God had remained faithful to his covenant promises. Paul addressed both groups and the tension of becoming one church in the midst of those differences.

In this letter, Paul wrote of the righteousness of God and the depth of his mercy, walking through humanity's need for saving grace – whether Jew or Gentile. He also explored justification by faith, life in the Spirit, and the transformation that comes from receiving his mercy. Paul frequently utilized Scriptures to show that God's work in Christ was the fulfillment of Old Testament promises spoken long ago.

As we explore these topics through the fifteen sessions in this book, you'll see that each session opens with warm-up introductory questions, has a selection from Romans and questions related to the passage. Then the study highlights the linked Old Testament passages and some reflection questions. Each study session ends with considerations for personal application. Additional tips and suggestions on approaching the study for individuals and groups follow.

Suggestions for this Study

This study is designed for individual or small group study and is composed of 15 sessions. It is designed to encourage thought and discussion of the scripture, encouraging individuals and groups seeking God to have conversations about the text. Jeremiah 29:13 states 'You will seek me and find me when you seek me with all your heart,' and the purpose of this study to help participants find the Lord and deepen their relationship with him.

General Guidelines for Individual Study

1. Open each session with prayer. Ask God to speak through his Word.

2. Respond to the introductory questions that focus on the theme of the session and what God says in the main reading.

3. Read the passage more than once, perhaps in different translations. Using different translations can offer expanded viewpoints on the meaning of the original text. This study uses the New International Version (NIV) as the basis of questions and quotes. However, any version may be used to provide insight and assist in revealing meaning.

4. This study is designed to offer a starting point for discovery of what God has to say to you through his Word. Because the study looks at how the Old Testament is reflected in the epistles, there are observation and interpretation questions about the readings in Romans and how they connect to the Old Testament. These are followed by application questions for personal reflection and group discussion. Writing your responses will provide clarity and focus your thoughts on the verses.

5. Use a Bible dictionary or other reference books to look up any unfamiliar words, places, or names.

General Guidelines for Group Study

1. Come to sessions prepared. Some groups will choose to read and respond ahead of time then gather and discuss together; others will gather to read and discuss together. Before beginning, agree how the group would like to proceed so everyone can be prepared.

2. Be an active participant in the group by sharing your thoughts and responses to the questions. Groups often have members who are in different places in their walk with Christ and each perspective should be valued.

3. Listen to each other. Consider the amount of time that is available for all to share and be careful not to dominate the conversation.

4. Be open-minded. Participants are encouraged to be open to learning and sharing, even expecting alternate viewpoints. The Bible serves as the foundation of this study and hearing other perspectives may challenge your own

understanding. When differing views arise, the focus should remain on listening to each other and encouraging one another to wrestle with difficult passages and concepts rather than building consensus. Full agreement about everything in Romans may be challenging at times given that it offers numerous key doctrines and complex passages that theologians have argued over for centuries.

5. Maintain group confidentiality. For participants to be willing to share and grow, the trust level in the group must be high. Do not share what is shared in the group outside of the group unless permission is given to do so.

6. Expect God to meet you in the study. His Word is living and active (Heb. 4:12) and he is present when we gather in his name (Matt. 18:20).

Introduction

Paul's letter to the Romans is often identified as one that addresses most specifically the path to salvation and justification. The letter addressed not only theological arguments, but also practical Christian living. Consider the following as a starting place for what God may reveal during the study.

What does the word "justify" mean in everyday language? How might that meaning differ in a biblical context?

How would you describe the relationship between belief and behavior? How does one influence the other?

Session 1: The Promised Gospel

Romans 1:1-17

Opening

Some households have a special set of dishes that are reserved for certain occasions. When are those dishes used and what makes those meals different?

What makes you confident in a message, cause, or belief? What helps you trust it enough to support it?

Paul's letter to the Romans opened with his expression of delight over the faithful Christians in Rome. His focus on the gospel and faith established a clear opening theme for the letter while also encouraging the believers. This emphasis provided a foundation for understanding Christ as the key figure of the gospel, shaping the letter and speaking to believers beyond its time and location and even to us today.

Read Romans 1:1-17.

Reading Questions

How did Paul describe the promised gospel?

How did Paul receive his apostleship?

How did Paul identify or describe the Romans in his greeting?

How did Paul pray for the Romans?

Why did Paul look forward to visiting the believers in Rome?

Romans 1:16-17 stated the theme of Romans. Identify three points that he made in these verses.

Old Testament Links

Paul's opening verses to the Romans laid out core aspects of the Gospel that would then outline the rest of the letter. He introduced righteousness in contrast to moral behavior, framing this righteousness as part of God's saving work. This understanding of righteousness was not new; it appeared in Genesis and continued through the Israelite story. Note how faith and righteousness were connected to God's saving acts for his people as you read the following passages.

Read Habakkuk 2:4 and Genesis 15:6. What is said about faithfulness and righteousness in these verses? Who was the actor? How does that compare to Romans 1:5?

Read Isaiah 51:5-8 and Psalm 98:1-3. Whose righteousness was offered and who brought salvation, according to these passages? What similarities do you notice in Romans 1:16-17?

Application

Paul greeted the Romans who belonged to Christ noting that they were loved and set apart. How does understanding yourself as already belonging to God and loved by Him shape the way you approach God? What questions, confirmations, or uncertainties does that raise for you?

Paul looked forward to the mutual encouragement of each other's faith (Romans 1:12). Is this something you have experienced? If so, describe it. If not, what groups might you consider joining to be encouraged through the faith of others?

Session 2: Revelation of God Himself

Romans 1:18–2:16

Opening

When something becomes important in a person's life, what signs may show that shift in priorities? What are some positive and negative examples?

What influences a person's sense of right or wrong over time?

Paul wasted no time turning to a contrast between God's revelation of himself and human behavior. As he described the ways people responded to that revelation, he included both Jews and Gentiles in his observations of human wrongdoing and judgment. Yet Paul also revealed glimmers of hope, acknowledging that those who pursued good would find blessing.

Read Romans 1:18–2:16.

Reading Questions

Who was God's wrath being revealed against?

What has God made plainly known?

Summarize what happened to those who suppressed the truth about God.

Which verses refer to the godless, which the wicked and which the religious?

According to the text, what leads to repentance?

What two groups of people will receive according to "what he has done"? What were their deeds and what will each group receive?

What did the law and sin have to do with Gentiles? What did the law and sin have to do with Jews?

Old Testament Links

Paul pulled ideas for this passage from the established Scriptures and dwelt on them. God's self-revelation and humanity's response to Him were already discussed in writings familiar to Paul's audience. While the Old Testament began with God's covenant with Israel, it also pointed outward, tracing a blessing designed to reach beyond one people to all nations. Within this design, Paul drew on the shared understanding that God's judgment and blessing were made available to all, Jew and Gentile, according to their deeds.

Read Ecclesiastes 3:11-17 and Psalm 98:1-6. According to these passages, what has God made known to humanity?

Read Habakkuk 2:4 and 2 Kings 5:1-14. What roots for Paul's ideas do you see in these passages?

Application

How does accountability for your actions influence the choices you make? Are there areas where this awareness of accountability has guided your decisions? Are there areas where it isn't but needs to?

Consider a specific time you were frustrated or critical of a loved one. How might this session's passage challenge the way you view that situation now?

Session 3: The Condition of Humanity

Romans 2:17–3:20

Opening

Schoolchildren sometimes label a rule-follower as a "goody two-shoes" or a "teacher's pet". How were rule-followers viewed by their peers and how might that perception change with age?

How does confidence in or knowledge of something influence behavior?

Paul continued the evaluation of the law and human actions in this passage. He called out hypocrisy and law breaking while again emphasizing the righteousness of God. This contrast finally culminated in his conclusion of humanity's condition.

Read Romans 2:17-3:20.

Reading Questions

Describe the kind of person Paul defined in Romans 2:17-23.

What was the result that came from that kind of person?

Compare and contrast the two kinds of circumcision.

What does Paul's contrast of man's sin and God's righteousness demonstrate?

What is Paul's conclusion?

What was the purpose of the law?

Old Testament Links

In Romans 1-3, Paul outlined the sinfulness and unrighteousness of humanity, addressing both Jews and Gentiles. In the middle of Romans 3, he concluded that all people were sinful and through the law became aware of their state. He undergirded this conclusion with numerous references from the Old Testament that reinforced his position.

Read Isaiah 59:7-8. How was human behavior described in these verses? What were the causes and results of those actions?

Read Psalm 14:1-3 and Psalm 36:1-4. What similarities do you see in these passages with what's in Romans 3:10-18? What is indicated about how humanity viewed God?

Application

Where have you seen the discrepancy between knowing what is right and consistently living it out in your own life?

In Romans 2:17-3:20, Paul compared Jews and Gentiles, finally declaring no one righteous (Romans 3:20). How does comparison influence the way you evaluate your own choices, for better or worse?

Session 4: Righteousness Credited

Romans 3:21-4:25

Opening

If someone paid a debt you could not repay, how might that affect the way you relate to that person?

What is the difference between trusting a promise and trusting the person who made the promise?

From the middle of Romans chapter 3, Paul presented God's response to the problem of sin and how people could approach God. He drew on the familiar relationship between God and Abraham to illustrate how righteousness was counted to him—not because of what he achieved, but because of his trust in God's promise. Paul placed Jews and Gentiles in the same condition and traced how blessing was extended beyond the Jewish people to all people.

Read Romans 3:21-4:25.

Reading Questions

Where does Paul say righteousness comes from? Who is it given to?

What actions did Paul attribute to God, according to verses 23-26?

How did God's actions show him both as a just God and a God who justifies?

According to Romans, was Abraham credited with righteousness before or after circumcision?

According to Romans 4:11-12, who was Abraham a father of? How did he receive this promise?

What was Abraham persuaded of regarding God?

To whom will God credit righteousness?

Old Testament Links

Paul leaned heavily on Old Testament texts for his examples of righteousness as gifted, drawing on both David and Abraham. The quote from one of David's psalms addressed sins no longer being counted, while Abraham's story traced how righteousness was gifted in the early Scriptures. Paul set aside lineage or performance as the basis for righteousness, and the focus moved toward God's promises and Abraham's trust.

Read Genesis 12:1-3, 15:1-6, and 16:1-4. Develop a timeline that includes both God's promises and actions as well as Abraham's actions. What do you note of the relationship between sin and righteousness in the timing of when righteousness was credited in Abraham's example?

Read Genesis 17:1-19, 21:1-5, 22:15-18 and Psalm 32:1-2. How was the passage from Psalms demonstrated through the account of Abraham?

Application

How does Abraham's relationship with God, with ups and downs of sin and righteousness, and of promise and fulfillment, impact your own sense of righteousness?

God's promise to Abraham was delayed over many years, yet God repeatedly renewed his promise. Is there something you are waiting for or hoping for right now? How does this passage speak on that waiting?

Session 5: Standing in Peace, Grace and Hope

Romans 5:1-21

Opening

In a workplace, a team might avoid conflict to maintain order. What is the difference between avoiding conflict and experiencing genuine peace within a team? What steps might help move a group from avoidance toward true peace?

Why does hope sometimes endure through hardship and at other times fade?

Romans 5 opened with Paul stating that justification by faith brought peace with God, access to grace, and hope in suffering. He highlighted Christ's death as a demonstration of God's love, through which relationship was restored or reconciled. He concluded this passage contrasting the actions and results of two men, emphasizing the transfer of power from sin and death to grace and life.

Read Romans 5:1-21.

Reading Questions

What did justification through faith bring?

How did Paul indicate believers could be certain of hope in suffering?

How was God's love demonstrated, according to Paul?

What brought about reconciliation with God?

In the second half of the chapter, Paul described the actions of two men who impacted God's world.

Complete the chart by identifying the actions of Adam and Christ as follows.

	Adam	Christ
What entered the world following his act?		
What was the immediate outcome of that act?		
What reign was the world put under because of that act?		

Complete the chart by identifying the actions of Adam and Christ.

Old Testament Links

In Genesis, the actions of one person, Adam, shaped the condition of many. Paul drew on the story familiar to his audience to show how Christ's actions functioned in a similar, yet more all-encompassing, way. By showing how one person's choices and activities impacted many, Romans 5:12-21 highlighted the consequences of a single action beyond the individual.

Read Genesis 3:17-24 and Romans 5:17-19. According to Genesis, how did the condition that Adam introduced spread? How did Paul contrast the extension of Christ's condition?

Read Genesis 2:16–17; 3:17–19; and Romans 5:15–17, 5:20–21. How did Paul acknowledge the results of Adam's sin and yet not let it have the final word?

Application

In the passage, Paul addressed consequences of a single act upon many. Consider an action you might have overlooked that had a major impact on others. How does that shape your view of responsibility?

Paul ended the discussion of transference, or being moved from the realm of sin to the realm of righteousness and life, with "…grace increased all the more," (Romans 5:20). How does knowing that God's grace not only covered but abounded impact your assurance of righteousness?

Session 6: Reign of Grace

Romans 6:1-23

Opening

What do people mean when they talk about freedom?

Is it possible to feel free while still being deeply committed or devoted to something? Explain why or why not.

Paul focused chapter 6 on two questions related to abundant grace: whether grace changed the reality of sin and what freedom meant once the law no longer ruled. He described the break from the old life and the transfer to a new one through participation in Christ's death and resurrection, drawing on the image of baptism. Freedom from sin was defined as release from one master and placement under another, as slaves to God. He ended the chapter by outlining the contrasting outcomes of lives lived under sin and under grace.

Read Romans 6:1–23.

Reading Questions

What impact does grace have upon sinning?

What are the two parts identified in the baptism and grace parallel?

What are the consequences of being raised to life?

What instruction did Paul give in Romans 6:12-13?

What did slavery to sin lead to? And slavery to righteousness?

How did Paul present sin as "work"?

Old Testament Links

Though Paul did not directly quote the Old Testament in this passage, he drew on long-standing scriptural themes of deliverance, belonging and life. These ideals shaped how life was defined in relationship with God. The contrasts Paul presented in Romans 6 showed continuity in God's desired relationship with man and the grace and life credited through Christ.

Read Deuteronomy 30:15-20. How were life and death described in Deuteronomy and Romans 6:1-14? How did Paul's use of slavery language relate to the kind of freedom described in Deuteronomy?

Read Proverbs 11:18-19 and Isaiah 55:1-3. How were the outcomes of sin and righteousness described in these passages? How did Paul summarize those outcomes in Romans?

Application

Paul described baptism as a death to the old and resurrection into new life. Yet he also acknowledged lingering sin. In what areas of your life do you find yourself still acting under that old influence?

Paul indicated that obedience led believers toward life and holiness. Where have you seen signs of this change of direction in your life?

Session 7: Rules that Break Us

Romans 7:1-25

Opening

People often make New Year's resolutions about health, habits, relationships, or work, yet still find themselves doing what they hoped to change or avoid. Why might that be?

Consider the example of wanting to respond calmly in a discussion but reacting defensively instead. How would you describe that experience of knowing what "should" be done while feeling pulled in the opposite direction at the same time.

Paul's discussion of grace contrasted with the law in chapters 6-8 culminated in the tension between desiring to do what is right and finding oneself unable to do so under one's own will. Paul described sin's activity while also illustrating the release of believers from the law through death, underscoring the inner struggle of humanity. The contrast and struggle were only lifted when Paul called upon the One who could deliver the believer.

Read Romans 7:1-25.

Reading Questions

What did the opening illustration demonstrate happened upon death?

For what reason did Paul give that the Romans "died to the law"?

What was the result of that death?

What was the purpose of the law?

How did Paul describe that the law was holy, righteous, and good?

Describe the contradiction within the one who seeks "to do what is right, but [has] not the ability to carry it out," (Romans 7:18).

Who can save believers from the "body of death"?

Old Testament Links

Paul's argument regarding the law was well established in Israelite literature. Paul used the foundational command of not coveting as an example in this discussion. His statements that obedience to the law was associated with life, yet resulted in death, reflected the tension present in Israel's engagement with the law and in their relationship with God.

Read Exodus 20:17 and consider how it illustrates Paul's point regarding the inner struggle of humanity.

Read Genesis 2:16-17, 3:6 and Leviticus 18:5. How were obedience and life described in these passages? What happened when the command was broken?

Read Exodus 20:1-17. How did the command against coveting differ from the other commandments? How did that particular command shape Paul's argument regarding humanity's inner struggle?

Application

Paul wrote that sin was active in destroying using words like "seizing" and "deceived," (Romans 7:11). Where have you felt that kind of activity in your life recently? How did that struggle unfold in the moment.

Paul said that he "delights in God's law," (Romans 7:22) though described inability to live it out. Where do you love what is good, but sense the pain of not being able to live it out? What does this reveal about your need for Christ?

Session 8: The Spirit Dwells in You

Romans 8:1-39

Opening

Occasionally we hear of someone imprisoned for years who is later found innocent and released. Imagine being that person and describe how you would feel and what you would do upon hearing that news.

How does belonging differ from being obligated to be in relationship?

Paul's final acclamation of chapter 7 became a declaration of freedom for those in Christ in this passage. He described life in the Spirit, contrasting those who live according to the flesh with those who live according to the Spirit. Paul continued by affirming adoption into sonship and future glory for those who belong to Christ. His closing phrases reminded the Romans that they were not alone, but dearly loved, as a truth that continues to shape believers today.

Read Romans 8:1-39.

Reading Questions

What explanation did Paul give for no condemnation for those who are in Christ?

How did Paul describe the benefits of receiving the Spirit?

Paul described creation as groaning. What reason did he give for that and when did he say it would stop?

How did Paul say the Spirit helps in weakness?

What progression did Paul outline in Romans 8:29-30, and how did it relate to his statement in verse 28?

What did Paul present as evidence that God is for believers?

What did he say could not separate believers from God's love?

Old Testament Links

Throughout Romans 8, Paul drew upon covenant language rooted in Israel's Scriptures. The promises God made formed the foundation of His relationship with His people in the Old Testament. Themes of covenant relationship and steadfast love shaped Paul's discussion as he addressed new believers loved by God.

Read Ezekiel 36:25-29. How was life under the renewed covenant described in the passage? Where did Paul use similar imagery in Romans 8?

Read Isaiah 54:10, Exodus 4:22, and Hosea 11:1.
Describe the relationship God had with Israel as
it is described in these passages. Compare that
relationship to the one Paul described in Romans 8.

Application

Paul declared there is no condemnation for those
in Christ Jesus. When you fail or fall short, what
is your first internal response? How does freedom
from condemnation change that response?

"Nothing …will be able to separate us from the love of God," Paul wrote in Romans 8:38-39. When do you find it hardest to believe this promise? Why?

Session 9: God is faithful

Romans 9:1-33

Opening

If you were playing a pickup game of volleyball or basketball and were the captain, what factors would guide your choice of members of your team?

When you hear the words "fair" and "merciful," do you think they always align? Why or why not?

Following the declaration of the inseparable love of God, Paul's earnest tone in Chapter 9 drew the reader into his question about Israel's story and

God's purposes. He asked whether God's word had failed, expressing deep grief that many of his fellow Israelites had not believed. God's promises had moved through specific lineages yet had always rested on mercy rather than human ancestry. Relationship with God is grounded in his covenant love and calling, topics that continued from Israel's Scriptures into Paul's discussion as today.

Read Romans 9:1-33.

Reading Questions

List the blessings that Paul named for the Israelites.

Which people did Paul indicate were children of God?

What explanation for God's choice to bless a specific lineage did Paul give?

How did Paul demonstrate the inclusion of Gentiles as well as Israelites into God's calling?

Which characteristics of God did Paul illustrate throughout Romans Chapter 9?

Old Testament Links

Paul utilized numerous scriptures from the Old Testament to trace the covenant love of God toward Israel and its application in Paul's day. The accounts from the patriarchs and prophets leaned on God's righteousness and mercy rather than the actions of any one individual. Paul's argument drew particularly on the relationship between Abraham and God, which informed how belonging to God was understood within his discussion in Romans 9.

Read Genesis 16:1-4, 17:15-21, and 21:1-12. How was the covenant promise clarified to Abraham across the encounters with God in these passages? What distinguished Isaac in relation to that promise? What did Paul emphasize about this in Romans 9?

What human questions or challenges did Abraham present in his discussions with God in these passages from Genesis? How did Paul draw attention to God's responses to those questions?

Application

Paul wrestled with how God's promises to Israel were unfolding in ways many people had not expected. Think of a time when events in your life developed very differently than you had planned. How did you respond to that change? What clarity would you still like to see about that change of plans?

Paul expressed deep grief for his fellow Israelites who had not believed, even while affirming God's purposes. Have you ever experienced sorrow for someone while still trusting God with their story? What did that reveal about your view of God?

Session 10: Faith Comes through Hearing

Romans 10:1-21

Opening

Think about the telephone game where a phrase or statement is whispered from one person to another. What tends to happen to the message as it moves around the group? What helps a message stay clear?

In what ways do people publicly identify with something – a team, belief, or cause? Why might someone hesitate to declare their identification with that group?

Turning from God's faithfulness in Chapter 9, Paul addressed humanity's response to that covenant and calling, particularly Israel's. Having presented that righteousness was not attained through lineage or law, but through faith, Paul described the promise of unearned righteousness and the proclamation of confession and belief in Christ. Faith, he said, came hearing the message of Christ.

Read Romans 10:1-21.

Reading Questions

What did Paul want for the Jews and how did he describe their zeal?

What two reasons did Paul give for Israel not submitting to God's righteousness?

What actions did Paul say were not required to obtain righteousness?

How did Paul illustrate the nearness of righteousness?

How did Paul describe the way a person is saved?

What action did Paul press the reader toward concerning the good news?

How did Paul say faith came to a person?

Old Testament Links

In Romans 10, Paul used extensive quotations from the Old Testament to convey the nearness of salvation and to address misunderstandings surrounding it. The passages from Deuteronomy highlight the accessibility of God's word and its placement within reach of the people. Paul echoed that language in describing the proclaimed message of Christ, presenting the saving word as near and ready to be heard. His extension of salvation beyond Israel alone to the Gentiles also found support in the Scriptures he drew upon.

Read Deuteronomy 30:11–14. How did Moses describe God's nearness? What did he explicitly say was not necessary to follow God? How did this passage together with Romans 10 emphasize the continuity of God's plan and desire for all to be saved?

In Deuteronomy, what was identified as "near"? In Romans 10, what did Paul identify as "near"? What difference did that shift reveal?

What similar language did the authors of Deuteronomy and Romans use to describe salvation? What did this suggest about the relationship between God's revealed Word and Jesus himself? How did this demonstrate Christ embodying the nearness described in Deuteronomy?

Application

When you sense weakness or failure in yourself, what tends to be your natural response? How does trusting Christ's righteousness reshape this response?

Paul wrote, "Everyone who calls in the name of the Lord will be saved," in Romans 10:13 What does calling on the Lord look like for you in everyday life? In what situations is it carried out and in what areas does it need to be?

Session 11: God's Commitment to His People

Romans 11:1-36

Opening

When a sports team loses a season, how do fans respond? What might cause some fans to remain loyal while others walk away?

Imagine a situation where an outcome took longer than expected, such as a promotion or car repair. How might people respond to a delay in these circumstances?

Paul continued his discussion of the salvation of Israel and the fulfillment of God's promises in Chapter 11. He emphasized the faithfulness of God throughout Israel's history and the preservation of a remnant. He turned then to an illustration of an olive tree to describe how both Gentiles and Jews were included in God's people. Repeatedly, Paul leaned into the promises of God and affirmed their reliability. He closed this passage with a doxology praising God's wisdom and greatness.

Read Romans 11:1-36.

Reading Questions

What evidence did Paul give that God had not rejected his people?

How did Paul say the remnant was chosen?

How did salvation and riches come to the Gentiles?

Describe the parts of the analogy: natural and wild olive branches, the root.

What warning did Paul give in the illustration of the olive tree?

What promise did Paul remind his readers of in
Romans 11:28-31?

Old Testament Links

Paul drew on passages that reminded the readers in
Rome of God's enduring faithfulness to his people
in the Scriptures. The historical account of Elijah
and the prophetic promise of redemption offered
insight into Paul's argument regarding Israel and the
consistent character of God.

Read about Elijah and the remnant in 1 Kings
19:9-18. Summarize Elijah's actions and God's
responses described in the passage. How did Paul
use this account in Romans 11?

Read Isaiah 59:20-21. What promise did these verses record? What aspects of that promise again appear in Romans 11?

Application

Paul warned Gentiles about arrogance in this chapter. Consider any areas of your spiritual life where you may be tempted to feel secure because of comparison rather than grace. How does Paul's reminder help maintain humility?

Walking in faith means that there's a lot that is happening that is invisible, yet Elijah was told that God was working behind the scenes. How does that example speak to your own struggle to trust God is working in the unseen?

Session 12: Transformed Living

Romans 12: 1-21

Opening

If your best friend or spouse received an unexpected gift of $25,000, what kind of response might they have?

In a volunteer group or community organization, what tends to happen when some members overestimate their role—or underestimate the value of their contribution?

Paul spent the first 11 chapters of his letter to the Roman church describing what God had done for believers. In this chapter, he turned to the natural response to that work: worship and loving others. His description of transformation moved into its expression within the church and in relationships with neighbors. His last exhortations in the chapter were to leave judgement to God while continuing to love.

Read Romans 12: 1-21.

Reading Questions

How did Paul describe the act of worship?

How were people to think of themselves?

Summarize Paul's comments on the body of Christ.

List the gifts of grace that Paul described. How should one respond to these gifts?

What characteristics did Paul use to describe love?

How should believers respond to evil?

Old Testament Links

Paul utilized the Scriptures of old to strengthen his call to love others. He urged the Romans to act in love toward one another, to leave judgement in God's hands, and to respond to enemies with unexpected kindness. These instructions were not new but were rooted in the Jewish Scriptures. The response to God's work found continuity in these earlier commands.

Read Leviticus 19:16-18 and Deuteronomy 32:35. How was neighborly behavior described in Leviticus? How did these passages hold together love and justice? How did Paul expand or illustrate neighborly love in Romans 12?

Read Proverbs 25:21-22. What result was anticipated when kindness was shown to the enemy? How did Paul frame this response in contrast to revenge?

Application

Paul said to "think of yourself with sober judgement," (Romans 12:3). Describe how you believe Christ sees you.

Consider your interactions this week and how you have honored others (Romans 12:10). In what ways did you live this out – or struggle to do so?

Session 13: Living in Integrity

Romans 13:1-14

Opening

What are some common attitudes toward taxation, both positive and negative?

How might citizenship relate to the way people treat one another?

Paul continued his call for transformed living, now addressing believers as members of society. He urged submission to governing authorities, describing civil government as part of God's providential order. Paul then returned to the central theme of love, stating that it fulfilled the law. He ended the passage with a reminder that salvation was nearer now than when the Romans first believed and he called them to live with alertness and integrity.

Read Romans 13:1-14.

Reading Questions

How did Paul describe God's interaction with government?

Summarize Paul's reasoning behind doing good.

What does a believer owe to others?

How did Paul say that love fulfilled the law?

Why had the time come to wake?

How did Paul summarize his recommendations to the Romans in Romans 13:14?

Old Testament Links

In Romans 13, Paul embraced the central tenants of Judaic law, referencing two key commands regarding human behavior. Though his teaching regarding governing authorities would have been challenging for his audience, his reminder of God's commands and their foundation in loving one another would have been familiar. The anchor of Scripture for Paul offered continuity, grounding civic responsibility and neighborly love in the law already given to Israel.

Read Deuteronomy 5:17–21. What pattern do you notice in the commands Paul cited? What area of life did they primarily address?

Read Exodus 20:13–17 and Leviticus 19:18. How did the individual commandments relate to the broader command to love your neighbor? How did Paul draw those threads together in Romans 13?

Application

The tension of living under the jurisdiction of governing authorities yet also of being called to a higher law existed in Paul's time as well. Describe a personal experience of living within that tension.

Paul urged believers to live as those aware that salvation is nearer than before. In what areas of your life do you sense complacency? What might it mean to live more attentively?

Session 14: Acceptance of One Another

Romans 14:1–15:13

Opening

People often celebrate holidays such as Easter or Christmas in different ways. What are some examples of these differences? How do people usually respond when others celebrate differently?

Think about the last time you were with a group ordering pizza. When people disagreed about toppings, how did that disagreement play out?

Paul addressed those of "weak" and "strong" faith in Romans 14:1-15:13, pointing to several issues that were disputable or not clearly settled in the Scriptures. Differences in conviction about food, special days, and personal practices had the potential to divide communities. Paul did not choose sides in these matters but instead urged believers to welcome one another and refrain from judging. He reminded them that each person stands before the Lord and urged the strong to limit their freedom for the sake of others. He also called them to love and humility, as Christ himself demonstrated, reminding his readers of the acceptance of both Gentiles and Jews into one unified community.

Read Romans 14:1–15:13

Reading Questions

How did Paul distinguish between those "whose faith is weak" and "strong"?

What did Paul say about how God views both groups?

Which two types of people did Paul say gave thanks to God?

Who stands before the judgement seat?

What is the kingdom of God a matter of?

Summarize how Paul urged believers to respond to disputes in these practical matters.

What reason did Paul give for acceptance of one another?

Old Testament Links

Questions of accountability before God and the inclusion of the nations were not new themes in Israel's Scriptures. Paul's appeal to welcome one another and to refrain from judgement rested on longstanding promises—such as the declaration that every knee will bow before God and the hope that the nations would trust in the Root of Jesse—which he quoted in this passage of Romans. His discussion of unity echoed the broader purposes of God revealed through the prophets.

Read Isaiah 45:22–25. What did the Lord declare about himself in this passage? What did this declaration suggest about ultimate accountability? How did Paul use this quotation in Romans 14?

Read Isaiah 11:1-3,10-16. Who was included in this vision? What response was anticipated? How did Paul draw on this passage in Romans 15?

Application

Describe a time when you chose not to exercise personal freedom for the sake of someone else. What did that cost you? What did it protect?

Where in your church or family do differences feel close to dividing lines? What does it look like to choose unity without compromising conscience?

Session 15: Faithful to Our Part

Romans 15:14–16:27

Opening

What different roles are necessary for the healthy functioning of an organization or church?

How does your organization or family celebrate success? How are various members of a team recognized?

Paul's final words to the Romans focused on the work that the faithful carried out for Christ. Beginning with his own ministry, he described the work of proclaiming the gospel and praised God for what had been accomplished through him. Paul became personal in this passage, expressing hope of visiting soon, but having been delayed. He urged prayer for his work and seeing one another again. He commended a great many friends and coworkers for the work of Christ among them. He closed by exhorting them to guard against divisions and praying for the revelation of Christ among all nations.

Read Romans 15:14–16:27.

Reading Questions

Why did Paul say he wrote this letter to the Romans?

What did Paul say he gloried in? What was his ambition?

Summarize Paul's plans and reasonings for them.

What was Paul's prayer request?

What were some of the similarities in Paul's greetings?

What final warning did Paul give, and what made him joyful?

Old Testament Links

As Paul concluded his letter, he again pointed to prophetic writings to describe the spread of the gospel. This promise reflected the ongoing vision of God's work. He maintained the central idea of God's work and saving grace through the Scriptures in his closing.

Read Isaiah 52:13-15. What did this passage anticipate regarding those who had not yet heard? How did Paul position his missionary work within that expectation?

How did both the passage from Isaiah and from Romans describe the revelation of what was once hidden? What did this suggest about the relationship between the prophetic writings and the proclamation of Christ?

Application

Paul described his mission as proclaiming the gospel to Gentiles which glorified God. In what ways does your daily life bring glory to God? What is your mission or role in Christ's work?

Identify three people that you work alongside, whether in family, workplace, or church activities and note what you would commend them for if you were to write a letter similar to Paul's. Consider sharing that encouragement with them this week.

Conclusion

Paul's letter to the Romans addressed God's righteousness and the depth of his mercy. The progression Paul presented of humanity's need for justification by faith to life in the Spirit and on to hope in future glory revealed God's consistent faithfulness to his established promises. Romans calls believers to trust in the gospel and to live transformed by mercy, walking in humility and unity with one another.

How has this study of Romans helped form your understanding of God's righteousness and mercy?

What have you learned about God's faithfulness?

What else did you learn about God from this study?

What did you learn about yourself from this study?

Do you believe that Jesus is the Messiah, the Son of God and have you received life in his name? If so, describe the qualities of that life.

If this is the first time that you have answered yes to the call of following Jesus, please reach out to a local church or the author to share of your choice and find support for your new life.

To continue your deep dive into "Seeing the Old Testament in the Epistles", pick up 1&2 Timothy: Guard the Faith to continue your study. Find it at your nearest retailer by scanning the QR code today.

1&2 Timothy
Bible Study

Also By Sarah K. Howley

Seeing the Old Testament in the Epistles
Ephesians: Experience God's Power
James: Know God's Wisdom
1&2 Thessalonians: Prepare for Christ's Return
Hebrews: Elevate Jesus
Philippians: Pursue Christ's Joy
1&2 Peter: Grow in Grace
Revelation: Worship the Lamb
Colossians & Philemon: Live Transformed
1,2&3 John: Dwell in Light
Romans: Trust the Faithful God

The Son Reveals the Father
I Am: An 8-Session Study of John
Heart: A 12-Session Study of Luke
Word: An 11-Session Study of Matthew
King: An 8-Session Study of Mark

Our Trustworthy God: How Much God loves You, Joyfully Engages with You, and Trusts You

Women of the Old Testament Bible Studies
Hope: A Bible Study of Women in Jesus' Lineage
Faith (coming 2026)
Love (coming 2026)

Alive Again Bible Study on Forgiveness
Alive Again: Find Healing in in Forgiveness
Alive Again Bible Study: Find Healing in Forgiveness
Alive Again Forgiveness Prayer Journal

About the Author

Author and founder of InspiritEncourage, Sarah K. Howley writes Bible studies that reveal the transforming depth of Scripture and lead readers into a thriving relationship with God. Known for weaving Old and New Testament connections with warmth and insight, she invites believers to encounter God's truth in everyday life. She fuels her writing with espresso—and gratitude for any gluten-free/dairy-free dessert she didn't bake herself. Sarah and her husband support global initiatives for literacy and hunger relief.

You can find Sarah on Facebook and Instagram @inspiritencourage. To book Sarah as a speaker at your next event, please contact her through her website. For weekly encouragement and

information on her latest releases, sign up for
Sarah's newsletter at InspiritEncourage.com.

InspiritEncourage